Yo...

I want to thank you ... ~~ying this~~ /ing this
book. To show my a ... ~~yether~~ -gether a free gift

Click Here to Download Your Free Book

www.stukkiesoftware.com/37-cheesecake-recipes

Just click the link to download your free gift.

I know you will love this gift!

Thank you!

Jennifer Connor

Introduction

Cheesecake is a delicious, sweet dessert, a dessert that your mother (maybe) is an expert at making. Well, it is time to dethrone her, and I'm going to help you do that.

Some people think that making cheesecake is near impossible, and opt to buy their cheesecakes (expensive!). Well, making cheesecake isn't impossible. In fact, the only thing you need to do is follow my recipes, and you will be surprised at how well you can make cheesecake.

What are the other benefits of making your own cheesecake? Well, that's pretty simple, too: you will save money and you will have fresher, tastier, cheesecake (even better than your mother's).

How to Use This Book

Throughout this book, you'll find tips and tricks, and obviously a recipe or two! Where to start? Well, the best way, in my humble opinion, is to look through the recipes and find the one that sounds the best to you. Then, get out a piece of paper, write down all of the ingredients that you need from the grocery store, and go buy them. Then, read through the Tips and Tricks section in this book.

Now, it's time to bake. Make sure you read the whole recipe, because I've added some secrets I've learned along the way that will make your cheesecake better than your mother's. When it's done, enjoy it, share it, and taunt your mother with it.

Table of Contents

Your Free Gift...1

Introduction..2

How to Use This Book 2

Cheesecake Tips and Tricks 5

Classic "New York" Cheesecake...7

Blueberry-Lemon Cheesecake 10

Pumpkin Cheesecake 13

Caramel Apple Cheesecake 16

Less-Fat Cheesecake...18

Crockpot Cheesecake with Gingersnap Crust 21

Red Velvet Cheesecake 23

Honey Ricotta Cheesecake 25

Peanut Butter Cheesecake 27

Carrot Cheesecake 29

Maple Pecan Pumpkin Cheesecake..32

Chocolate Peanut Butter Cheesecake 35

White Chocolate Raspberry Cheesecake....................................37

Key Lime Cheesecake 39

Goat Cheese Cheesecake..42

Vegan Lemon Raspberry Cheesecake...44

Coconut and Blackberry Ricotta Cheesecake 46

Banana-Coffee Cheesecake 48

Coconut and Raspberry Cheesecake 50

Lemon-Orange Cheesecake 52

Chocolate Orange Cheesecake 54

Salted Caramel Cheesecake...56

Ginger Cheesecake 58

Marbled Chocolate Cheesecake...60

No-bake Chocolate Cheesecake...63

Strawberry Yogurt Cheesecake..65

Layered Turtle Cheesecake...67

Oreo™ & Reese's™ Cheesecake 70

Cafe Mocha Cheesecake Recipe...73

Double Berry Cheesecake on Phyllo Crust 77

White Chocolate Lemon Cheesecake 79

Low Sugar Cheesecake 81

Chocolate Chip Cookie Dough Cheesecake 83

Honey Cheesecake 85

Pomegranate-Glazed Orange Cheesecake 87

Bailey's™ Irish Cream Cheesecake 90

Kahlúa™ Chocolate Cheesecake 93

So, how did it go?...95

Cheesecake Tips and Tricks

Have you ever thought: "Cheesecake is too expensive and too complicated to make"

This is a common fear among bakers who have not attempted to make cheesecake before. Or, among those who have never attempted baking at all! But, the good news, this fear couldn't be more wrong!

Have you ever noticed how expensive it is to buy cheesecake? Making your own cheesecake will cut your cost in half (if not more).

Plus, the whole process is simpler than it appears. Ever heard the saying "if you can read, you can cook"? Well, that's exactly what this book is for!

Follow these simple tricks to make each recipe easier:

General Tips:
Start with all ingredients at room temperature.

Do NOT over-mix! Cheesecakes are supposed to be rich and heavy - over mixing will cause it to be more light and fluffy.

Stop that crack!
Cracking of the cheesecake is caused by quick temperature changes. So, cool slowly. Start by cooling at room temperature before placing the cake in the fridge.

You will notice the recipes in this book suggest running a thin spatula around the edge after you remove the cake from the oven. This loosens the cake from the sides to prevent cracking as it cools.

Mix it up!

Do not be afraid to experiment with different types of cheeses. See the Honey Ricotta Cheesecake recipe, or try your own creation. Neufchatel, cottage cheese, fromage blanc, and mascarpone are all possible alternatives.

You can make a "lighter" version of any cheesecake but using low-fat cream cheese or substituting in ricotta cheese.

Freezing?

Yes! You can freeze your cheesecake to extend its life! Just wrap it tightly and freeze for up to 2 weeks (but, if your cheesecake has higher water content - like those with fruit - it may not freeze as well).

Classic "New York" Cheesecake

Everyone loves a creamy slice of classic cheesecake. Cheesecake is so delicious, there is often no need for fancy additions. For a more adventurous take on this cake, try any type of fruit topping by following the simple topping recipe included!

Total Time: 5 hours & 45 minutes.
Prep time: 30 minutes

Yields: 1 9-inch cheesecake
Level: Easy

Ingredients:
Crust:
1¾ cups graham cracker crumbs
3 tbsp light brown sugar

½ tsp ground cinnamon
½ cup melted butter

Pie Filling:
2 (8-ounce) packages cream cheese, at room temperature
3 eggs
1 cup sugar
1 pint sour cream
1 lemon, zested
1 dash vanilla extract

Optional Topping:
1 pint fruit (blueberries, raspberries, strawberries, etc.)
2 tbs sugar

Directions:
Preheat oven to 325°F.

To make crust:
In a medium bowl, use a fork to mix together the graham cracker crumbs, sugar, and cinnamon. Then, add the melted butter and mix well. Press mixture into a 9-inch springform pan coated with cooking spray. Set aside until needed.

To make filling:
With an electric mixer or stand mixer, beat cream cheese until smooth. Gradually add sugar and beat until smooth. Add vanilla, sour cream, and lemon zest. Mix well but do not over-beat.

Pour entire mixture into the prepared crust and spread evenly. Smooth with a spatula.

To bake:
Set cake pan on top of aluminum foil and wrap foil around sides. Place cake pan in a large roasting pan. Add enough boiling water to the roasting pan so that the water is about

halfway up the cake pan (the aluminum foil prevents water from reaching cake).

Bake in preheated oven for 45 minutes. Cheesecake will be jiggly and will firm upon cooling, so do not over cook. Run a thin spatula around the inside rim. Let cool for 30 minutes, then chill in refrigerator for 4 hours.

To make optional topping:
Combine berries and sugar in a small saucepan. Simmer on low heat until fruit begins to break down and sauce forms. Allow to cool.

Remove cake from springform pan and transfer to cake plate. Pour topping over cheesecake. Slice with a knife dipped in warm water for smooth cuts.

Blueberry-Lemon Cheesecake

Rich, creamy cheesecake paired with the perfect combination of a sweet and refreshing blueberry-lemon topping. What could be better? You can best enjoy a slice on your deck while sipping lemonade on a beautiful summer day.

Total Time: 5 hours & 45 minutes.
Prep time: 30 minutes

Yields:1 9-inch cheesecake
Level: Easy

Ingredients:
Crust:
1¾ cups graham cracker crumbs
3 tbsp light brown sugar
½ tsp ground cinnamon
½ cup melted butter

Pie Filling:
2 (8-ounce) packages cream cheese, at room temperature
3 eggs
1 cup sugar
1 pint sour cream
1 lemon, zested
1 dash vanilla extract

Warm Blueberry-Lemon Topping:
1 pint fresh blueberries
1 lemon, zested and juiced
2 tbsp sugar

Directions:

Preheat the oven to 325 degrees F.

To make crust:

In a medium bowl, use a fork to mix together the graham cracker crumbs, sugar, and cinnamon. Then, add the melted butter and mix well. Press mixture into a 9-inch springform pan coated with cooking spray. Set aside until needed.

To make filling:

With an electric mixer or stand mixer, beat cream cheese until smooth. Add eggs, 1 at a time. Beat until combined. Gradually add sugar and beat until creamy.

Add vanilla, sour cream, and lemon zest. Mix until smooth, but do not over beat.

Pour entire mixture into the prepared crust and spread evenly. Smooth with a spatula.

To bake:

Set cake pan on top of aluminum foil and wrap foil around sides. Place cake pan in a large roasting pan. Add enough boiling water to the roasting pan so that the water is about halfway up the cake pan (the aluminum foil prevents water from reaching cake).

Bake in preheated oven for 45 minutes. Cheesecake will be jiggly and will firm upon cooling, so do not over cook. Let cool for 30 minutes, then chill in refrigerator for 4 hours.

Run a thin spatula around the inside rim. Remove from springform pan and transfer to cake plate.

To make warm blueberry-lemon topping:

Add all ingredients in a saucepan and simmer over medium heat for 5 minutes. Let cool.

Use a spatula to spread the warm blueberry-lemon topping over the top of the cake. Slice with a knife dipped in warm water for smooth cuts.

Pumpkin Cheesecake

Are you looking for a new way to incorporate pumpkin into your fall treats? This Pumpkin Cheesecake is the perfect way to incorporate your favorite fall flavor into a rich, creamy cake. It is sure to be a favorite at your next fall gathering!

Total Time: 5 hours & 30 minutes
Prep Time: 15 minutes

Yield: 1 9-inch cheesecake
Level: Easy

Ingredients:
Crust:
1¾ cups graham cracker crumbs
3 tbsp light brown sugar
½ tsp ground cinnamon
½ cup melted butter

Pie Filling:

3 (8 ounce) packages cream cheese, at room temperature
1 (15 ounce) can pureed pumpkin
3 eggs plus 1 egg yolk
¼ cup sour cream
1½ cups sugar
½ teaspoon ground cinnamon
⅛ teaspoon ground nutmeg

Directions:

Preheat oven to 350ºF.

To make crust:
In a medium bowl, use a fork to mix together the graham cracker crumbs, sugar, and cinnamon. Then, add the melted butter and mix well. Press mixture into a 9-inch springform pan coated with cooking spray. Set aside until needed.

To make filling:
With an electric mixer or stand mixer, beat cream cheese until smooth. Next, add pumpkin, sugar, sour cream, eggs, egg yolk, cinnamon, and nutmeg. Once combined, add flour and vanilla. Continue mixing until well combined.

Pour entire mixture into the prepared crust and spread evenly. Smooth with a spatula.

To bake:
Set cake pan on top of aluminum foil and wrap foil around sides. Place cake pan in a large roasting pan. Add enough boiling water to the roasting pan so that the water is about halfway up the cake pan (the aluminum foil prevents water from reaching cake).

Bake in preheated oven for 1 hour. Cheesecake will be jiggly and will firm upon cooling, so do not overcook. Let cool for 15 minutes, then chill in refrigerator for 4 hours.

Run a thin spatula around the inside rim. Remove from springform pan and transfer to cake plate. Slice with a knife dipped in warm water for smooth cuts.

Caramel Apple Cheesecake

Are you looking for something different for your family to enjoy this fall? Try pairing a fall favorite with a rich and creamy cheesecake. Your guests will love this caramel apple treat!

Total Time: 56 Minutes
Prep Time: 20 minutes

Yield: 1 9-inch cheesecake
Level: Intermediate

Ingredients:
Crust:
1¾ cups graham cracker crumbs
3 tbsp light brown sugar
½ tsp ground cinnamon
½ cup melted butter

Pie Filling:
2 (8-ounce) packages cream cheese, at room temperature
1 (21-ounce) can apple pie filling
¼ cup caramel topping
½ cup sugar
1 tsp vanilla extract
2 eggs
12 pecan halves, plus 2 tbsp chopped pecans

Directions:
Preheat the oven to 350 degrees F.

To make crust:

In a medium bowl, use a fork to mix together the graham cracker crumbs, sugar, and cinnamon. Then, add the melted butter and mix well. Press mixture into a 9-inch springform pan coated with cooking spray.

Spoon ¾ of the can of apple pie filling into the crust. Set aside until needed.

To make filling:
Add the remaining ¼ can apple pie to a small saucepan. Mix in caramel topping. Heat on low until melted.

With an electric mixer or stand mixer, beat cream cheese until smooth. Add eggs, 1 at a time. Beat until combined. Gradually add sugar and vanilla.

Pour entire mixture into the prepared crust over top the apple pie filling. Smooth with a spatula.

To bake:
Set cake pan on top of aluminum foil and wrap foil around sides. Place cake pan in a large roasting pan. Add enough boiling water to the roasting pan so that the water is about halfway up the cake pan (the aluminum foil prevents water from reaching cake).

Bake in preheated oven for 35 minutes. Cheesecake will be jiggly and will firm upon cooling, so do not over cook. Let cool to room temperature.

Use a spatula to spread apple-caramel mixture on top of the cheesecake. Sprinkle chopped pecans on cake and decorate the edge with pecan halves. Chill in refrigerator for 4 hours.

Run a thin spatula around the inside rim. Remove from springform pan and transfer to cake plate. Slice with a knife dipped in warm water for smooth cuts.

Less-Fat Cheesecake

True, you can not truly eliminate all the calories from a rich and creamy cheesecake. But, we all need *some* calories, right? Try cutting down on some of the guilt by cutting out some of the fat… but not too much!

Total Time: 2 hours &10 minutes
Prep Time: 1 hour

Yield: 1 9-inch cheesecake
Level: Intermediate

Ingredients:
Crust:
1¾ cups graham cracker crumbs
3 tbsp light brown sugar
½ tsp ground cinnamon
½ cup melted butter

Pie Filling:
2 (8-ounce) packages Neufchatel cream cheese, at room temperature.
2 (8-ounce) packages fat-free cream cheese, at room temperature
1½ cups sugar
1 cup reduced-fat sour cream
2 large eggs plus 3 egg whites
2 tbsp all-purpose flour
1 tsp vanilla extract
1 tsp finely grated lemon zest
Assorted toppings

Directions:

Preheat the oven to 350 degrees F.

To make crust:

In a medium bowl, use a fork to mix together the graham cracker crumbs, sugar, and cinnamon. Then, add the melted butter and mix well. Press mixture into a 9-inch springform pan coated with cooking spray. Bake until browned, about 8 minutes.

To make filling:

With an electric mixer or stand mixer, beat both cream cheeses until smooth. Gradually add sugar until smooth. Beat in sour cream. Whisk 3 egg whites in another bowl. Then, add cheese mixture, 2 eggs, flour, lemon zest, and vanilla. Beat until smooth.

Pour entire mixture into the prepared crust over top the apple pie filling. Smooth with a spatula.

To bake:

Set cake pan on top of aluminum foil and wrap foil around sides. Place cake pan in a large roasting pan. Add enough boiling water to the roasting pan so that the water is about halfway up the cake pan (the aluminum foil prevents water from reaching cake).

Bake in preheated oven for 1 hour and 10 minutes. Cheesecake will be jiggly and will firm upon cooling, so do not over cook. Turn oven off, and keep cheesecake inside with the door closed for 20 minutes.

Remove from water bath and transfer to a cooling rack. Run a thin spatula around the inside rim. Let cool to room temperature. Chill in refrigerator for 8 hours.

Remove from springform pan and transfer to cake plate. Add toppings if desired. Slice with a knife dipped in warm water for smooth cuts.

Crockpot Cheesecake with Gingersnap Crust

Are you loving all the combination dinners you can make with your slow cooker? Get ready for this one - cooking your next cheesecake in your slow-cooker! No need to worry about a dry cake, this method will create a moist, creamy cheesecake every time.

Total Time: 9 hours &10 minutes
Prep Time: 10 minutes

Yield: 1 9-inch cheesecake
Level: Intermediate

Ingredients:
Crust:
24 gingersnap cookies
¼ cup plus 1 tbsp unsalted butter, melted
salt

Filling:
2 (8-ounce) packages cream cheese, at room temperature
1 cup lightly-packed light brown sugar
¾ cup pumpkin puree
¼ cup sour cream
2 tsp vanilla extract
1 tsp pumpkin pie spice
3 large eggs, at room temperature

Directions:

Using a large piece of aluminum foil, loosely roll a 1-inch cylinder about 20 inches long. Form a 7-inch diameter ring with the foil. Fill your slow cooker with ½ inch of water and place the foil ring at the bottom.

To make crust:

Add ginger snaps to a food processor and make small crumbs. Add ¼ cup melted butter and a pinch of salt. Continue to pulse mixture until it looks like wet sand.

Brush a 9-inch springform pan with melted butter and press the crumb mixture into the bottom and halfway up the pan sides.

In a medium bowl, use a fork to mix together the graham cracker crumbs, sugar, and cinnamon. Then, add the melted butter and mix well. Press mixture into a 9-inch springform pan coated with cooking spray.

To make filling:

With an electric mixer, food processor, or stand mixer, beat cream cheese until smooth. Add brown sugar until smooth. Combine pumpkin puree, vanilla, sour cream, and pumpkin pie spice until smooth. Add eggs until uniform.

Pour entire mixture into the prepared crust. Smooth with a spatula.

To bake:

Place the cheesecake on the foil ring in the slow-cooker. Place paper towel under the lid. Cook on low heat for 4 hours and then allow it to cool in the slow cooker for 2 hours.

Remove cheesecake and run a thin spatula around the inside rim. Cover with plastic. Refrigerate for at least 3 hours.

Remove from springform pan and transfer to cake plate.

Red Velvet Cheesecake

Are you looking to create a birthday surprise for your dad who loves Red Velvet Cake? Or, maybe it is just a favorite of yours? Try this spin on Red Velvet by incorporating the classic dessert into cheesecake form.

Total Time: 9 hours &10 minutes
Prep Time: 10 minutes

Yield: 1 9-inch cheesecake
Level: Intermediate

Ingredients:
Crust:
1 ½ cups finely crushed chocolate wafer cookies (about 28 cookies)
5 tbsp unsalted butter, melted
⅓ cup sugar
Pinch of salt

Pie filling:
4 (8-ounce) packages cream cheese, at room temperature
1 ¼ cups sugar
1 tbsp fresh lemon juice
1 tsp vanilla extract
2 tbsp flour
4 large eggs
1 tbsp unsweetened cocoa powder
1 tsp red food coloring

Directions:

Preheat the oven to 350°F.

To make crust:

In a medium bowl, use a fork to mix together the cookie crumbs, sugar, salt, and melted butter. Press mixture into a 9-inch springform pan coated with cooking spray. Bake until set, about 10 minutes.

To make filling:

Reduce oven to 325°F. With an electric mixer, or stand mixer, combine cream cheese, sugar, lemon juice and vanilla until smooth. Gradually add flour and eggs until smooth.

Transfer 2 cups of mixture to a medium bowl. Add cocoa and food coloring, mix until smooth. Add this mixture onto the crust. Then, pour the remaining white batter over top. Use a spoon to pull some of the red batter up top and swirl.

Bake in preheated oven for 1 hour and 20 minutes. Cheesecake will be jiggly and will firm upon cooling, so do not over cook. Turn oven off, and keep cheesecake inside with the door closed for 20 minutes.

Run a thin spatula around the inside rim. Let cool to room temperature. Chill in refrigerator for 4 hours.

Remove from springform pan and transfer to cake plate. Add toppings if desired. Slice with a knife dipped in warm water for smooth cuts.

Honey Ricotta Cheesecake

With so many delicious cheeses out there, why limit your cheesecakes to just cream cheese? Try adding some ricotta cheese for a new twist on your traditional cheesecakes recipes that won't disappoint.

Total Time: 1 hour & 50 minutes
Prep Time: 20 minutes

Yield: 1 9-inch cheesecake
Level: Intermediate

Ingredients:
Crust:
8 ounces biscotti
6 tsp (3/4 stick) unsalted butter, melted

Pie Filling:
1 (12-ounce) container fresh whole milk ricotta, drained
2 (8-ounce) packages cream cheese,at room temperature
¾ cup sugar
¼ cup orange blossom or clover honey
1 tbsp orange zest
4 large eggs

Directions:
Preheat the oven to 350ºF.

To make crust:
Finely grind the biscotti in a food processor. Use a fork to mix in the melted butter. Press mixture into a 9-inch springform pan coated with cooking spray. Bake until browned, about 15 minutes. Allow to cool completely.

To make filling:
With an electric mixer, food processor, or stand mixer, beat ricotta until smooth. Add cream cheese and sugar until smooth. Blend in honey and orange zest. Gradually add the eggs until smooth. Do not over mix.

Pour entire mixture over prepared crust.

To bake:
Set cake pan on top of aluminum foil and wrap foil around sides. Place cake pan in a large roasting pan. Add enough boiling water to the roasting pan so that the water is about halfway up the cake pan (the aluminum foil prevents water from reaching cake).

Bake in preheated oven for 1 hour and 5 minutes. Cheesecake will be jiggly and will firm upon cooling, so do not over cook. Let cool for 1 hour, then chill in refrigerator for 8 hours.

Run a thin spatula around the inside rim. Remove from springform pan and transfer to cake plate.

Peanut Butter Cheesecake

For those peanut butter lovers in your life, this cheesecake is packed with goodness. From a peanut butter crust, to a creamy peanut butter filling - each bite is truly perfect.

Total Time:
Prep Time:

Yield: 1 9-inch cheesecake
Level: Easy

Ingredients:
Crust:
10 peanut butter cookies
1 tsp sugar
3 tbsp melted butter

Filling:
1 ½ cups granulated sugar
2 pounds cream cheese
4 large eggs
1 cup creamy peanut butter
1 tbsp flour
2 tsp vanilla extract
Powdered sugar

Directions:
Preheat the oven to 350°F.

To make crust:

Finely grind the peanut butter cookies in a food processor. Use a fork to mix in the melted butter, and tsp of sugar. Press mixture into a 9-inch springform pan coated with cooking spray. Bake until browned, about 15 minutes. Allow to cool completely.

To make filling:
With an electric mixer or stand mixer, beat cream cheese and peanut butter until smooth. Combine sugar and flour until smooth. Gradually add eggs and vanilla until well combined. Do not over mix.

Pour entire mixture over prepared crust.

To bake:
Set cake pan on top of aluminum foil and wrap foil around sides. Place cake pan in a large roasting pan. Add enough boiling water to the roasting pan so that the water is about halfway up the cake pan (the aluminum foil prevents water from reaching cake).

Bake in preheated oven for 2 hours. Cheesecake will be jiggly and will firm upon cooling, so do not over cook. Let cool for 1 hour, then chill in refrigerator for 8 hours.

Run a thin spatula around the inside rim. Remove from springform pan and transfer to cake plate. Dust with powdered sugar.

Carrot Cheesecake

This spring, try out a new combination for your favorite carrot cake recipe. Simply follow our carrot cake recipe, or use your favorite. The, top with a delicious layer of cheesecake. This recipe adds a whole new twist to the cream cheese frosting we all love about carrot cake!

Total Time: 2 hours
Prep Time: 30 minutes

Yield: 1 9-inch cheesecake
Level: Intermediate

Ingredients:
Carrot Cake:
½ cup pecan halves, plus more, chopped, for garnish
1 cup all-purpose flour
1 tsp baking powder
¾ tsp baking soda
1 tsp ground cinnamon
½ tsp ground ginger
Kosher salt
½ cup vegetable oil
½ cup sugar
2 large eggs
1½ cups shredded carrot (2 to 3 medium carrots)

Cheesecake:
3 (8-ounce) packages cream cheese, softened
⅔ cup sour cream
⅔ cup granulated sugar
3 large eggs
3 tbsp flour
1 tsp lemon zest plus 2 tbsp lemon juice (from 1 lemon)
1 tsp vanilla extract

Sour Cream Topping:
½ cup confectioners' sugar
2 tbsp sour cream
¼ tsp pure vanilla extract
Pinch salt

Directions:
Preheat the oven to 350ºF.

To make carrot cake:
Spread ½ cup pecans on a baking sheet and bake until toasted (10-12 minutes). Allow to cool. Then chop.

In a large bowl, mix chopped pecans, flour, baking soda, baking powder, ginger, cinnamon, and ¼ tsp salt.

In a medium bowl, whisk oil, sugar, and eggs. Add shredded carrots. Fold this mixture into the flour mixture until well combined.

Pour into a 9-inch spring form cake pan. Bake 20-25 minutes. Cool completely.

To make cheesecake:
With an electric mixer or stand mixer, beat cream cheese, sour cream, and sugar until smooth. Combine sugar and flour until smooth. Gradually add eggs until well combined. Mix in flour, vanilla, lemon zest and lemon juice until just combined.

Pour entire mixture over carrot cake.

To bake:
Set cake pan on top of aluminum foil and wrap foil around sides. Place cake pan in a large roasting pan. Add enough boiling water to the roasting pan so that the water is about

halfway up the cake pan (the aluminum foil prevents water from reaching cake).

Bake in preheated oven for 1 hour. Cheesecake will be jiggly and will firm upon cooling, so do not over cook. Turn off oven and let cool for 30 minutes in the hot oven. Run a thin spatula around the inside rim. Let cook on a wire rack. Then, cover and chill in refrigerator for 8 hours.

Remove from springform pan and transfer to cake plate.

For the sour cream topping:
Whisk the sour cream, confectioners' sugar, salt and vanilla until smooth. Spread on top of the cheesecake. Garnish with chopped pecans and refrigerate for 30 minutes.

Maple Pecan Pumpkin Cheesecake

Are you a maple lover looking for any excuse to add the delicious flavor to your treats this fall? This cheesecake is the perfect mix of pumpkin and maple. Top is off with toasted pecan crumbles and you will have a new fall favorite!

Total Time: 10 hours & 25 minutes
Prep Time: 20 minutes

Yield:1 9-inch cheesecake
Level: Intermediate

Ingredients:

Crust:
1¾ cups graham cracker crumbs
3 tbsp light brown sugar
½ tsp ground cinnamon
½ cup melted butter

Filling:
3 (8-ounce) packages cream cheese, at room temperature
3 large eggs, at room temperature
1 (15-ounce) can pure pumpkin puree (not pumpkin pie filling)
1 (14-ounce) can sweetened condensed milk
3 tbsp pure grade B maple syrup
2 tsp ground cinnamon
1 tsp ground nutmeg
½ tsp fine sea salt

Maple Pecan Glaze:
1 cup heavy cream
⅔ cup pure grade B maple syrup
¾ cup toasted pecan pieces

Directions:
Preheat the oven to 350°F.

To make crust:
In a medium bowl, use a fork to mix together the graham cracker crumbs, sugar, and cinnamon. Then, add the melted butter and mix well. Press mixture into a 9-inch springform pan coated with cooking spray.

To make filling:
With an electric mixer or stand mixer, beat cream cheese until smooth. Add eggs and mix. Gradually add pumpkin puree, maple syrup, and sweetened condensed milk until smooth. Add cinnamon, nutmeg, and salt. Beat until light and fluffy.

Pour entire mixture into prepared crust.

To bake:
Set cake pan on top of aluminum foil and wrap foil around sides. Place cake pan in a large roasting pan. Add enough boiling water to the roasting pan so that the water is about halfway up the cake pan (the aluminum foil prevents water from reaching cake).

Bake in preheated oven for 1 hour and 15 minutes. Cheesecake will be jiggly and will firm upon cooling, so do not over cook. Cool for 1 hour. Run a thin spatula around the inside rim. Let cook on a wire rack. Then, cover and chill in refrigerator for 4 hours.

Remove from springform pan and transfer to cake plate.

For the glaze:

Combine cream and maple syrup in a medium sauce pan and bring to a boil. After thickened, about 25 minutes, stir in pecan pieces. Cover and chill.

To serve:
Stir chilled clase and spoon over cheesecake.

Chocolate Peanut Butter Cheesecake

There is no doubt about it, chocolate and peanut butter at a match made in heaven! Add that delicious pair to a creamy cheesecake and you will never look back. Absolutely perfect!

Total Time: 1 hour & 15 minutes
Prep Time:30 minutes

Yield: 1 9-inch cheesecake
Level: Easy

Ingredients:
Crust:
2 cups graham cracker crumbs
½ cup salted peanuts
½ cup bittersweet chocolate chips
4 tbsp soft unsalted butter

Filling:
2 (8-ounce) packages cream cheese, at room temperature
3 eggs
3 egg yolks
1 cup superfine sugar
½ cup sour cream
1 cup creamy peanut butter

Topping:
1 cup sour cream
1 cup milk chocolate chips
2 tbsp light brown sugar

Directions:

Preheat the oven to 350°F.

To make crust:

Use a food processor to finely combine graham crackers, peanuts, bittersweet chocolate, and butter. Press mixture into a 9-inch springform pan coated with cooking spray. Let sit in refrigerator.

To make filling:

With an electric mixer or stand mixer, beat all filling ingredients until smooth. Pour entire mixture into prepared crust.

To bake:

Set cake pan on top of aluminum foil and wrap foil around sides. Place cake pan in a large roasting pan. Add enough boiling water to the roasting pan so that the water is about halfway up the cake pan (the aluminum foil prevents water from reaching cake).

Bake in preheated oven for 1 hour. Cheesecake will be jiggly and will firm upon cooling, so do not over cook. Run a thin spatula around the inside rim. Let cook on a wire rack.

To make topping:

In a small saucepan, warm sour cream, brown sugar, and milk chocolate over low heat. Gently whisk as heating. Spread topping over cheesecake and put back in oven for 10 minutes.

Then, cover and chill in refrigerator for 4 hours.

Remove from springform pan and transfer to cake plate.

White Chocolate Raspberry Cheesecake

Are you a white chocolate lover trying to find more recipes to add to your collection? The almonds in this crust pair perfectly with the white chocolate filling. Mixed with fresh raspberries and you will have a new favorite!

Total Time: 4 hours & 25 minutes
Prep Time: 30 minutes

Yield: 1 9-inch cheesecake
Level: Intermediate

Ingredients:
Crust:
1 cup slivered almonds
2 cups graham cracker crumbs
¼ cup unsalted butter, melted
Filling:
4 (8-ounce) packages cream cheese, at room temperature
8 ounces fine-quality white chocolate
½ cup plus 2 tablespoons sugar
4 whole large eggs
2 large egg yolks
2 tbsp flour
1 tsp vanilla
2 cups fresh raspberries

Garnish: Fresh raspberries, mint sprigs and raspberry coulis

Directions:

Preheat the oven to 350°F.

To make crust:

Use a food processor to finely chop almonds and graham crackers. Add butter and mix with a fork. Press mixture into a 9-inch springform pan coated with cooking spray. Let sit in refrigerator.

To make filling:

Using a double boiler, melt chocolate until smooth.

With an electric mixer or stand mixer, beat cream cheese until smooth. Add sugar until smooth. Gradually mix in eggs and yolks. Beat in flour and vanilla until combined, do not over mix. Then, gradually add melted chocolate while beating.

Lay berries in 1 layer over crust. Pour filling over berries.

Bake 40-45 minutes, until cake is slightly jiggly. Run a thin spatula around the inside rim. Let cook on a wire rack. Then, cover and chill in refrigerator for 4 hours.

Key Lime Cheesecake

The refreshing taste of key lime meet the creamy goodness of cheesecake in this blended recipe. Surprise your favorite key lime-lover or make it as a treat for yourself. Either way you won't be disappointed with the eclectic mix of flavors that hit your tongue.

Total Time:
Prep Time:

Yield: 1 9-inch cheesecake
Level: Intermediate

Ingredients:
Crust:
1¾ cups graham cracker crumbs
3 tbsp light brown sugar
½ tsp ground cinnamon
½ cup melted butter

Filling:
1¼ cups sugar, plus ¼ cup
1 cup graham cracker crumbs
1 envelope unflavored gelatin
¾ cup key lime juice
4 eggs, at room temperature
2 egg yolks, at room temperature
2 tablespoons grated key lime zest
1 (8-ounce) package cream cheese, at room temperature
2 egg whites, at room temperature
Pinch of salt
2 cups sweetened whipped cream

1 cup simple syrup (1 cup sugar, 1 cup water heated until sugar dissolves)
Rind of 2 limes, julienned

Directions:

To make crust:
In a medium bowl, use a fork to mix together the graham cracker crumbs, sugar, and cinnamon. Then, add the melted butter and mix well. Press mixture into a 9-inch springform pan. Set aside.

To make filling:
Using a medium saucepan and medium heat, dissolve gelatin in the key lime juice. Add 1¼ cups sugar, egg yolks, eggs, and lime zest. Cook until mixture is a pudding texture, about 10 minutes. Remove from heat.

With an electric mixer or stand mixer, beat cream cheese until smooth. Gradually add lime mixture until smooth. Cover mixture and allow to cool in a refrigerator. Mix every 10 minutes.

Using the whip attachment of an electric mixer, whip egg whites, salt, and ¼ cup sugar until stiff peaks form. Remove lime and cheese mixture from refrigerator, fold egg whites into mixture and blend well.

Pour entire mixture into prepared crust. Cover, and refrigerate for 4 hours.
Run a thin spatula around the inside rim of cheesecake.
Spread whipped cream over top of cake.

For candied zest:

Over medium heat, combine simple syrup and lime zest in a saucepan. Allow it to simmer for 3-4 minutes, then cool on parchment paper. Use to garnish cake.

Goat Cheese Cheesecake

Are you just dying to switch up the usual cream cheese mix?
Goat cheese adds the perfect amount of flavor and
creaminess to this cheesecake recipe. Paired with a
gingersnap crust and it is the perfect combo.

Total Time: 13 hours & 30 Minutes
Prep Time:20 Minutes

Yield: 1 9-inch cheesecake
Level: Intermediate

Ingredients:
Crust:
2 cups gingersnap crumbs
6 tbsp melted butter
¼ cup sugar
Pinch salt

Filling:
2 (8-ounce) packages cream cheese, at room temperature
1 (12-ounce) log goat cheese
12 ounces sour cream
4 eggs
1 cup sugar
2 tsp vanilla extract

Directions:
Preheat the oven to 350°F.

To make crust:

In a medium bowl, use a fork to mix all crust ingredients. Press mixture into a 9-inch springform pan coated with cooking spray. Set aside.

To make filling:
With an electric mixer or stand mixer, beat cream cheese and goat cheese until smooth. Gradually add sour cream until combined. Slowly add eggs and beat after each addition until well combined. Last, beat in sugar and vanilla.

Pour entire filling into prepared crust.

To bake:
Set cake pan on top of aluminum foil and wrap foil around sides. Place cake pan in a large roasting pan. Add enough boiling water to the roasting pan so that the water is about halfway up the cake pan (the aluminum foil prevents water from reaching cake).

Bake in preheated oven for 55 minutes. Cheesecake will be jiggly and will firm upon cooling, so do not over cook. Remove from oven and let cool on wire rack. Run a thin spatula around the inside rim. Then, cover and chill in refrigerator for 4 hours.

Remove from springform pan and transfer to cake plate.

Vegan Lemon Raspberry Cheesecake

There is no need to sacrifice on a vegan diet - we have your cheesecake craving covered! This delicious recipe comes with a coconut-almond--date crust that you may start adding to all your recipes.

Total Time:
Prep Time:

Yield: 1 9-inch cheesecake
Level: Intermediate

Ingredients:
Crust:
3 cups almonds
1 cup medjool dates, pitted
½ cup coconut, shredded
Pinch sea salt
2 tbsp coconut oil (liquid form)

Pie Filling:
3½ cups cashews
1 cup (full) lemon juice
⅔ cup agave, maple syrup, coconut nectar or date paste
½ cup coconut oil (liquid form)
2 tsp vanilla extract
zest of 2 lemons
1 punnet raspberries (fresh or frozen)
Pinch sea salt

Garnish
fresh raspberries
sprinkling of almond and date base

Directions:

To make crust:
In a food processor, finely chop nuts and salt. Add dates, coconut oil and shredded coconut and blend. Set a small amount aside for garnish. Press remaining mixture into a 9-inch springform pan. and place in freezer.

To make filling:
Place all filling ingredients in a food processor and finely blend until smooth. Pour mixture into pie crust and freeze for 2 hours. You can also choose to fold raspberries into mixture before pouring over crust.

All cake to thaw for 30 minutes before serving. Garnish, and serve.

Coconut and Blackberry Ricotta Cheesecake

Did you try, and love, the Honey Ricotta Cheesecake Recipe? Well, there is no reason to stop there. The coconut and blackberry additions in this recipe pair perfectly with the creamy ricotta filling. You will begin to wonder why you have not always used ricotta cheese in your cakes!

Cook Time: 1 hour & 15 minutes
Prep time: 15 minutes

Yield: 1 9-inch cheesecake
Level: Easy

Ingredients

Crust:
1¾ cups graham cracker crumbs
3 tbsp light brown sugar
½ tsp ground cinnamon
½ cup melted butter

Filling:
1 large container (2lb 2oz) ricotta
7oz Greek coconut yogurt
1 cup sugar
1tbsp corn flour, sifted
3 large eggs, beaten
1¾ cup blackberries
Icing sugar to dust

Directions:

Preheat the oven to 325ºF.

To make crust:

In a medium bowl, use a fork to mix together the graham cracker crumbs, sugar, and cinnamon. Then, add the melted butter and mix well. Press mixture into a 9-inch springform pan. Set aside.

To make filling:

In a large bowl, whisk sugar, ricotta, yogurt, corn flour, and eggs until well combined. Fold in half the blackberries.

Pour entire mixture into crust. Bake 1 hour and 25 minutes. Allow to cool and run a thin spatula around the inside rim. Refrigerate for at least 2 hours.

Top with remaining blackberries. Dust with icing sugar and serve.

Banana-Coffee Cheesecake

Coffee-lovers beware! One bite of this cheesecake and you will begin craving it as part of your breakfast routine! It pairs perfectly with a steamy cup of your favorite coffee blend. Plus, it has bananas - so it is a solid breakfast, *right*?

Total Time: 6 hour & 30 minutes
Prep time: 25 minutes

Yield: 8 servings
Level: Easy

Ingredients

Crust:
8 ounces biscotti
6 tbsp (3/4 stick) unsalted butter, melted

Filling:
2 small very ripe bananas, about 5oz, peeled
1 (8-ounce) package cream cheese, room temperature
1 cup sugar
1½ tbsp flour
1 tsp vanilla extract
2 medium eggs, separated

Topping:
3 tbsp caramel sauce
1 ounce plain chocolate shavings

Directions:

Preheat the oven to 350ºF.

To make crust:

Finely grind the biscotti in a food processor. Use a fork to mix in the melted butter. Press mixture into a 9-inch springform pan coated with cooking spray. Bake until browned, about 15 minutes. Allow to cool completely.

To make filling:

Finely mix bananas in food processor, or with an electric mixer until smooth. Add remaining filling ingredients except for egg whites. Mix well.

In a separate bowl, whip egg whites until the hold stiff peaks. Fold into banana mixture.

Pour entire mixture into crust.

To bake:

Set cake pan on top of aluminum foil and wrap foil around sides. Place cake pan in a large roasting pan. Add enough boiling water to the roasting pan so that the water is about halfway up the cake pan (the aluminum foil prevents water from reaching cake).

Bake in preheated oven for 50 minutes. Cheesecake will be jiggly and will firm upon cooling, so do not over cook. Let cool for 15 minutes, then run a thin spatula around the inside rim. Chill in refrigerator for 4 hours.

Remove from springform pan and transfer to cake plate. Drizzle caramel over top and sprinkle chocolate. Slice with a knife dipped in warm water for smooth cuts.

Coconut and Raspberry Cheesecake

This delicious pair of coconut and raspberry are part of a cheesecake recipe that you won't have to bake! Once the crust is set, simply fill it up and refrigerate. You will love this simple addition to your next summer gathering.

Total Time: 8 hours & 25 minutes
Prep Time: 25 Minutes

Yield: 1 9-inch cheesecake
Level: Easy

Ingredients
Crust:
1¾ cups graham cracker crumbs
3 tbsp light brown sugar
½ tsp ground cinnamon
½ cup melted butter

Pie Filling:
½oz powdered raspberry gelatin
2 (8-ounce) packages cream cheese, at room temperature
1¾ cup double cream
1¾ cup (14 ounces) coconut milk
1 cup sugar, sifted
2 cups raspberries
1 tbsp dried coconut

Directions:
Preheat the oven to 350°F.

To make crust:

In a medium bowl, use a fork to mix together the graham cracker crumbs, sugar, and cinnamon. Then, add the melted butter and mix well. Press mixture into a 9-inch springform pan coated with cooking spray. Bake until golden (15 minutes). Set aside until needed.

To make filling:
In a small bowl, mix gelatin with 4 tbsp boiled water. Stir until dissolved and set aside.

With an electric mixer or stand mixer, beat cream cheese until smooth. Mix in cream, coconut milk and sugar. Mix until smooth and thickened.

Beat in gelatin mixture and half the raspberries.

Pour entire mixture into the prepared crust and spread evenly. Smooth with a spatula. Place remaining berries on top as a garnish. Chill for at least 0 hours in refrigerator.

Lemon-Orange Cheesecake

Are you looking for a refreshing summer dessert to enjoy over an ice cold lemonade? This Lemon-Orange Cheesecake will do just the trick. It is the perfect combination of sweet and refreshing. You and your guests will love it!

Total Time: 6 hours & 10 Minutes
Prep Time:30 Minutes

Yield: 1 9-inch cheesecake
Level: Easy

Ingredients
Crust:
1¾ cups graham cracker crumbs
3 tbsp light brown sugar
½ tsp ground cinnamon
½ cup melted butter

Pie Filling:
2 (8-ounce) packages of cream cheese, at room temperature
1 cup cream
¾ cup plus 2 tbsp sugar
4 eggs
grated rinds of 1 lemon and 1 orange

Directions:
Preheat oven to 300ºF.

To make crust:
In a medium bowl, use a fork to mix together the graham cracker crumbs, sugar, and cinnamon. Then, add the melted

butter and mix well. Press mixture into a 9-inch springform pan coated with cooking spray. Set aside until needed.

To make filling:
With an electric mixer or stand mixer, beat cream cheese, eggs and sugar until smooth. Fold in cream and rinds.

Pour entire mixture into the prepared crust and spread evenly. Smooth with a spatula.

To bake:
Set cake pan on top of aluminum foil and wrap foil around sides. Place cake pan in a large roasting pan. Add enough boiling water to the roasting pan so that the water is about halfway up the cake pan (the aluminum foil prevents water from reaching cake).

Bake in preheated oven for 55 minutes. Cheesecake will be jiggly and will firm upon cooling, so do not over cook. Turn off and let stand in oven for half an hour. Let cool for 15 minutes, then run a thin spatula around the inside rim. Chill in refrigerator for 4 hours.

Remove from springform pan and transfer to cake plate. Slice with a knife dipped in warm water for smooth cuts.

Chocolate Orange Cheesecake

For all you chocolate-lovers out there, here is a flavor combo that you are sure to love. Chocolate and orange have been used in combination for ages - why not try it out in a cheesecake? You will love the contrasting flavors and creamy filling.

Total Time: 13 hours & 30 Minutes
Prep Time:20 Minutes

Yield: 1 9-inch cheesecake
Level: Easy

Ingredients:

Crust:
1¾ cups chocolate graham cracker crumbs
3 tbsp light brown sugar
½ cup melted butter

Filling:
2 (8-ounce) packages of cream cheese, at room temperature
¾ cup sour cream
1 cup sugar
1½ tbsp flour
1 tsp vanilla extract
Zest of 1 orange
2 medium eggs, separated

Garnish:
5 ounces chocolate flakes

Directions:

Preheat oven to 350°F.

To make crust:

In a medium bowl, use a fork to mix together the graham cracker crumbs, sugar, and cinnamon. Then, add the melted butter and mix well. Press mixture into a 9-inch springform pan coated with cooking spray. Set aside until needed.

To make filling:

With an electric mixer or stand mixer, beat all filling ingredients except egg whites. Mix until smooth. Whisk egg whites in separate bowl until stiff peaks appear. Fold egg whites into cheese mixture.

Pour entire mixture into the prepared crust and spread evenly. Smooth with a spatula.

To bake: Set cake pan on top of aluminum foil and wrap foil around sides. Place cake pan in a large roasting pan. Add enough boiling water to the roasting pan so that the water is about halfway up the cake pan (the aluminum foil prevents water from reaching cake).

Bake in preheated oven for 35-40 minutes. Cheesecake will be jiggly and will firm upon cooling, so do not over cook. Let cool for 15 minutes, then run a thin spatula around the inside rim. Chill in refrigerator for at least 2 hours.

Remove from springform pan and transfer to cake plate. Sprinkle with chocolate flakes. Slice with a knife dipped in warm water for smooth cuts.

Salted Caramel Cheesecake

For a luxurious cheesecake experience, this salted caramel filling will do just the trick. The sprinkled sea salt over top caramel syrup and caramel filling leave your mouth craving another bite.

Total Time: 9 hours & 20 Minutes
Prep Time: 50 Minutes

Yield: 1 9-inch cheesecake
Level: Intermediate

Ingredients
Crust:
1¾ cups graham cracker crumbs
3 tbsp light brown sugar
½ tsp ground cinnamon
½ cup melted butter

Filling:
3 (8 oz) packages cream cheese, at room temperature
1 cup packed brown sugar
3 eggs
¾ cup whipping cream
¼ cup caramel-flavored coffee syrup

Caramel Sauce:
½ cup butter
1¼ cups packed brown sugar
2 tablespoons caramel-flavored coffee syrup
½ cup whipping cream
1 ½ teaspoons flaked sea salt

Directions:

Preheat oven to 300°F.

To make crust:

In a medium bowl, use a fork to mix together the graham cracker crumbs, sugar, and cinnamon. Then, add the melted butter and mix well. Press mixture into a 9-inch springform pan coated with cooking spray. Set aside until needed.

To make filling:

With an electric mixer or stand mixer, beat cream cheese, and brown sugar until smooth. Gradually beat in eggs until combined. Add whipping cream and coffee syrup until blended.

Pour entire mixture into the prepared crust and spread evenly. Smooth with a spatula.

To bake: Set cake pan on top of aluminum foil and wrap foil around sides. Place cake pan in a large roasting pan. Add enough boiling water to the roasting pan so that the water is about halfway up the cake pan (the aluminum foil prevents water from reaching cake).

Bake in preheated oven for 1 hour and 10 minutes. Cheesecake will be jiggly and will firm upon cooling, so do not over cook. Turn off and let sit in oven for 30 minutes. Then, let cool on cooling rack for 30 minutes, then run a thin spatula around the inside rim. Chill in refrigerator for 6 hours.

To make caramel sauce:

In a small saucepan, melt butter. Add brown sugar and coffee syrup and heat to a boil. Cook and stir until sugar dissolves, about 1 minute. Add whipping cream and return to a boil. Remove from heat and let cool for 10 minutes. Drizzle caramel sauce and sprinkle with salt.

Ginger Cheesecake

The flavour of ginger is a delicious compliment to a sweet, creamy cheesecake. This cake offers a ginger crust, with both fresh and crystallized ginger in the cake filling. The recipe adds an exciting twist to your traditional cheesecake experience.

Total Time: 9 hours & 40 Minutes
Prep Time: 30 Minutes

Yield: 1 9-inch cheesecake
Level: Easy

Ingredients:

Crust:
2 cups gingersnap crumbs
3 Tbs. granulated sugar
7 Tbs. unsalted butter, melted

Pie filling:
3 (8-oz). packages cream cheese, at room temperature
¾ cup sour cream
2 tbs all-purpose flour
Pinch table salt
1¼ cups granulated sugar
2 tbs finely chopped crystallized ginger
2 tbs finely chopped fresh ginger
1 tbs pure vanilla extract
4 large eggs, at room temperature

Directions:

Preheat oven to 370ºF.

To make crust:
In a medium bowl, use a fork to mix together the gingersnap crumbs, sugar, and melted butter. Press mixture into a 9-inch springform pan coated with cooking spray. Bake until crust is slightly dark (9-12 minutes). Set aside to let cool.

Reduce oven to 300ºF.

To make filling:
With an electric mixer or stand mixer, beat cream cheese until smooth. Gradually add sour cream, flour and salt until well combined. Add sugar and blend well. Next, add both gingers and vanilla until just combined. Gradually add eggs. Do not over beat.

Pour entire mixture into the prepared crust and spread evenly. Smooth with a spatula.

To bake: Set cake pan on top of aluminum foil and wrap foil around sides. Place cake pan in a large roasting pan. Add enough boiling water to the roasting pan so that the water is about halfway up the cake pan (the aluminum foil prevents water from reaching cake).

Bake in preheated oven for about 55 minutes. Cheesecake will be jiggly and will firm upon cooling, so do not over cook. Let cool for 15 minutes, then run a thin spatula around the inside rim. Chill in refrigerator for 8 hours.

Remove from springform pan and transfer to cake plate. Slice with a knife dipped in warm water for smooth cuts.

Marbled Chocolate Cheesecake

This classic style cake makes for a delicious cheesecake too!
Your guests will enjoy both the taste and presentation of this
cheesecake. Plus, the marble effect is a cinch to create!

Total Time: 5 hours & 40 minutes
Prep Time: 30 minutes

Yield: 1 9-inch cheesecake
Level: Easy

Ingredients:

Crust:
1¾ cups chocolate graham cracker crumbs
3 tbsp light brown sugar
½ cup melted butter

Pie Filling:
3 packages (8 oz. each) cream cheese, at room temperature
1 cup sugar, divided
½ cup sour cream
2½ tsp vanilla extract, divided
3 tbsp all-purpose flour
3 eggs
¼ cup cocoa
1 tbsp vegetable oil

Directions:

Preheat oven to 350°F.

To make crust:
In a medium bowl, use a fork to mix together the graham cracker crumbs, and sugar. Then, add the melted butter and mix well. Press mixture into a 9-inch springform pan coated with cooking spray. Set aside until needed.

To make filling:
With an electric mixer or stand mixer, beat cream cheese until smooth. Add sour cream, ¾ cup sugar, and 2 tsp vanilla until well combined. Gradually add flour. Beat in eggs, one at a time.

In a second bowl, mix cocoa and remaining ¼ cup sugar. Add oil, ½ tsp vanilla and 1½ cups of the cream cheese mixture. Beat until smooth.

Pour plain and chocolate batters over crust in an alternating fashion. Gently swirl with a knife to create marble effect.

To bake: Set cake pan on top of aluminum foil and wrap foil around sides. Place cake pan in a large roasting pan. Add enough boiling water to the roasting pan so that the water is about halfway up the cake pan (the aluminum foil prevents water from reaching cake).

Bake in preheated oven for 55 minutes. Cheesecake will be jiggly and will firm upon cooling, so do not over cook. Let cool for 15 minutes, then run a thin spatula around the inside rim. Chill in refrigerator for 4 hours.

Remove from springform pan and transfer to cake plate. Slice with a knife dipped in warm water for smooth cuts.

No-bake Chocolate Cheesecake

Don't you hate turning on your stove on a hot summer day? Now, your taste buds do not have to suffer along with the heat! Try this no-bake cheesecake so that you can still enjoy a delicious, creamy dessert without heating up your house in the process.

Total Time: 3 hours & 20 Minutes
Prep Time: 20 Minutes

Yield: 1 9-inch cheesecake
Level: Easy

Ingredients:

Crust:
1¾ cups graham cracker crumbs
3 tbsp light brown sugar
½ tsp ground cinnamon
½ cup melted butter

Pie Filling:
2 (8-ounce) packages of cream cheese, at room temperature
1 14-ounce can (1¼ cups) sweetened condensed milk
¼ cup fresh lemon juice
1 tsp vanilla extract

Directions:

Preheat oven to 350ºF.

To make crust:
In a medium bowl, use a fork to mix together the graham cracker crumbs, sugar, and cinnamon. Then, add the melted butter and mix well. Press mixture into a 9-inch springform pan coated with cooking spray. Set aside until needed.

To make filling:
With an electric mixer or stand mixer, beat cream cheese until smooth. Slowly add condensed milk. Then beat in lemon and vanilla until smooth.

Pour entire mixture into the prepared crust and spread evenly. Smooth with a spatula. Refrigerate for 3 hours.

Remove from springform pan and transfer to cake plate. Slice with a knife dipped in warm water for smooth cuts.

Strawberry Yogurt Cheesecake

Guess what? Yogurt is a great way to flavor your basic cheesecake recipe! This Strawberry Yogurt Cheesecake is delicious. And, it is easily adjustable… try substituting blueberry yogurt and fresh blueberries. Or, peach yogurt and fresh peaches. The options are endless!

Total Time: 13 hours & 30 Minutes
Prep Time: 25 Minutes

Yield: 1 9-inch cheesecake
Level: Easy

Ingredients:

Crust:
1¾ cups graham cracker crumbs
3 tbsp light brown sugar
½ tsp ground cinnamon
½ cup melted butter

Pie Filling:
2 (8-ounce) packages of cream cheese, at room temperature
2 cups strawberry yogurt
1¼ cup heavy cream
1¼ cup strawberries, tops removed and slice
2 tbsp icing sugar

Directions:

To make crust:

In a medium bowl, use a fork to mix together the graham cracker crumbs, sugar, and cinnamon. Then, add the melted butter and mix well. Press mixture into a 9-inch springform pan coated with cooking spray. Set aside until needed.

To make filling:
With an electric mixer or stand mixer, beat yogurt and cream cheese until smooth.

Whip the heavy cream in a bowl until firm peaks form. Fold the cream into the cream cheese mixture.

Pour entire mixture into the prepared crust and spread evenly. Smooth with a spatula. Chill in refrigerator for 3 hours.

When ready to serve, arrange slices strawberries around edge.

Layered Turtle Cheesecake

Caramel, chocolate, and nuts. A delicious combo. Now, add that to the savory taste of cheesecake and you have the perfect dessert. This cheesecake will be your new favorite.

Total Time: 13 hours & 30 Minutes
Prep Time: 40 Minutes

Yield: 1 9-inch cheesecake
Level: Hard

Ingredients

Crust:
1 cup all-purpose flour
⅓ cup packed brown sugar
¼ cup finely chopped pecans
6 tbsp cold butter, cubed

Pie filling:
4 packages (8 ounces) cream cheese, at room temperature
1 cup sugar
⅓ cup packed brown sugar
¼ cup plus 1 tsp flour, divided
2 tbsp heavy whipping cream
1½ tsp vanilla extract
4 eggs, lightly beaten
½ cup milk chocolate chips, melted and cooled
¼ cup caramel ice cream topping
⅓ cup chopped pecans

Topping:
½ cup milk chocolate chips

¼ cup heavy whipping cream
2 tbsp chopped pecans

Directions

Preheat oven to 325°F.

To make crust:
Using a fork, mix flour, brown sugar, pecans, and butter until crumbly. Press mixture into a 9-inch springform pan coated with cooking spray. Bake for 12 minutes. Allow to cool.

To make filling:
With an electric mixer or stand mixer, beat cream cheese and sugars until smooth. Add ¼ cup flour, vanilla, and heavy cream. Gradually add eggs until just blended.

A 1 cup of cheese mixture to a small bowl and stir in melted chocolate. Spread over prepared crust.

In a medium bowl, mix caramel and remaining flour. Add pecans. Using a tablespoon, drop over chocolate batter on crust.

Add remaining cheese mixture over top.

To bake: Set cake pan on top of aluminum foil and wrap foil around sides. Place cake pan in a large roasting pan. Add enough boiling water to the roasting pan so that the water is about halfway up the cake pan (the aluminum foil prevents water from reaching cake).

Bake in preheated oven for 1 hour and 20 minutes. Cheesecake will be jiggly and will firm upon cooling, so do not over cook. Let cool for 15 minutes, then run a thin spatula around the inside rim. Chill in refrigerator for 4 hours.

To make topping:
In a small saucepan, bring cream to a boil. Set chocolate chips in a bowl and pour boiling cream over top. Stir until smooth. Allow to cool slightly while stirring occasionally.

Remove cake from springform pan and spread ganache over cake. Sprinkle with pecans; refrigerate until set. Drizzle caramel overtop. Slice with a knife dipped in warm water for smooth cuts.

Oreo™ & Reese's™ Cheesecake

Even the crust of this cake is packed with flavor! From an oreo crust, to a Reese's topping, everyone will go crazy for this cheesecake! It will be the hit of your next party.

Ingredients

For the crust:
1¼ cups graham cracker crumbs
¼ cup sugar
¼ cup crushed cream-filled chocolate sandwich cookies
6 tbsp butter, melted
¾ cup creamy peanut butter

For the filling:
3 packages (8 ounces) cream cheese, at room temperature
1 cup sugar
1 cup (8 ounces) sour cream
1½ tsp vanilla extract

3 eggs, lightly beaten
1 cup hot fudge ice cream topping, divided
6 peanut butter cups, cut into small wedges

Directions

Preheat oven to 350°F.

To Make Crust:
Use a fork to mix graham cracker crumbs, sugar, cookie crumbs, and butter. Press mixture into a 9-inch springform pan coated with cooking spray. Bake for 8 minutes. Allow to cool.

Heat peanut butter in the microwave until softened (about 30 seconds). Spread over prepared crust keeping it 1 inch away from the edge.

To make filling:
With an electric mixer or stand mixer, beat cream cheese and sugar until smooth. Add sour cream and vanilla. Gradually add eggs until just combined. Pour 1 oup of this mixture into a bowl and set aside.

Pour remaining mixture over peanut butter layer on crust.

Heat ¼ cup fudge in the microwave until warm (about 30 seconds). Fold into cream cheese mixture that was set aside. Pour over cake and swirl with a knife.

To bake:
Set cake pan on top of aluminum foil and wrap foil around sides. Place cake pan in a large roasting pan. Add enough boiling water to the roasting pan so that the water is about halfway up the cake pan (the aluminum foil prevents water from reaching cake).

Bake in preheated oven for 55 minutes. Cheesecake will be jiggly and will firm upon cooling, so do not over cook. Let cool for 15 minutes, then run a thin spatula around the inside rim.

Microwave remaining fudge a spread over cake before serving. Garnish with peanut butter cups. Chill in refrigerator for 4 hours.

Remove from springform pan and transfer to cake plate. Slice with a knife dipped in warm water for smooth cuts.

Cafe Mocha Cheesecake Recipe

Are you craving a Mocha Latte on that cold winter day? Try your mocha - cheesecake style! This cheesecake comes with an Oreo crust, a chocolate cheesecake layer, and a coffee cheesecake layer. It's awesome!

Total Time: 13 hours & 30 Minutes
Prep Time: 30 Minutes

Yield: 1 9-inch cheesecake
Level: Easy

Ingredients

For the crust:
1½ cups Oreo cookie crumbs
¼ cup butter, melted

For the filling:
4 packages (8 ounces each) cream cheese, at room temperature
2 tbsp plus 1½ tsp instant coffee granules
1 tbsp hot water
¼ tsp ground cinnamon
1½ cups sugar
¼ cup all-purpose flour
2 tsp vanilla extract
4 eggs, lightly beaten
2 cups (12 ounces) semisweet chocolate chips, melted and cooled

For the topping:
½ cup semisweet chocolate chips
3 tbsp butter
Chocolate-covered coffee beans (optional)

Directions:

Preheat oven to 325°F.

To make crust:
In a medium bowl, use a fork to mix together cookie crumbs and butter. Press mixture into a 9-inch springform pan coated with cooking spray. Set aside until needed.

To make filling:
In a small bowl, mix coffee granules, cinnamon, and hot water. Set aside.

With an electric mixer or stand mixer, beat cream cheese sugar and vanilla until smooth. Gradually beat in flour, mixing well. Add eggs and beat until just combined.

Divide mixture in half. Stir melted chocolate into one half and pour over prepared crust.

In the other half of the mixture, stir in coffee mixture. Pour over chocolate layer.

To bake:
Set cake pan on top of aluminum foil and wrap foil around sides. Place cake pan in a large roasting pan. Add enough boiling water to the roasting pan so that the water is about halfway up the cake pan (the aluminum foil prevents water from reaching cake).

Bake in preheated oven for 60 minutes. Cheesecake will be jiggly and will firm upon cooling, so do not over cook. Let cool for 15 minutes, then run a thin spatula around the inside rim. Chill in refrigerator for 6 hours.

Remove from springform pan and transfer to cake plate. Slice with a knife dipped in warm water for smooth cuts.

To make topping:
Melt chocolate chips and butter in a microwave. Stir until smooth and spread over cheesecake. Garnish with chocolate covered coffee beans if desired.

Double Berry Cheesecake on Phyllo Crust

Are you looking for something unique to make for dessert? This cheesecake has a phyllo crust! It goes perfectly with the berry-filled cheesecake filling. A perfect addition to your summer barbecue.

Total Time: 13 hours & 30 Minutes
Prep Time: 20 Minutes

Yield: 1 9-inch cheesecake
Level: Easy

Ingredients

For the crust:
8 sheets phyllo dough (14 inches x 9 inches)
6 tablespoons butter, melted

For the filling:
2 packages (8 ounces) cream cheese, at room temperature
½ cup sugar
1 tsp vanilla extract
2 eggs, lightly beaten
2 cups fresh or frozen blueberries
½ cup strawberry jelly
1 cup whipped topping
Sliced fresh strawberries and additional blueberries, optional

Directions:

Preheat oven to 425°F.

To make crust:
Grease a 9-inch springform pan. Place 1 phyllo sheet on the pan and brush with melted butter. Repeat 7 times. Trim edges and cover. Bake for 7 minutes or until light brown. Allow to cool on wire rack.

Lower oven to 350°F.

To make filling:
With an electric mixer or stand mixer, beat cream cheese until smooth. Add sugar and vanilla until smooth. Gradually add eggs until just combined. Fold in blueberries.

Pour entire mixture into the prepared crust and spread evenly.

To bake:
Bake for 10 minutes. Then, cover edges with foil (to prevent browning) and bake for an additional 25 minutes. Cheesecake will be jiggly and will firm upon cooling, so do not over cook. Let cool for 15 minutes, then run a thin spatula around the inside rim. Chill in refrigerator for 6 hours.

Remove from springform pan and transfer to cake plate. Slice with a knife dipped in warm water for smooth cuts.

To make topping:
In a small bowl, beat jelly until smooth and spread over cheesecake. Add whipped topping with a spatula until smooth. Garnish with additional strawberries and blueberries if desired.

White Chocolate Lemon Cheesecake

Even the crust of this cake is perfect! With a little added lemon peel, the crust goes perfectly with the white chocolate, lemon cheesecake filling. It is both savory and refreshing at the same time!

Total Time: 7 hours & 25 Minutes
Prep Time: 30 Minutes

Yield: 1 9-inch cheesecake
Level: Easy

Ingredients:

Crust:
1¼ cups all-purpose flour
2 tbsp confectioners' sugar
1 tsp grated lemon peel
½ cup cold butter, cubed

Pie filling:
4 (8 ounce) packages cream cheese, at room temperature
1¼ cups sugar
10 ounces white baking chocolate, melted and cooled
2 tbsp all-purpose flour
2 tbsp heavy whipping cream
2 tbsp lemon juice
2 tsp grated lemon peel
2 tsp vanilla extract
4 eggs, lightly beaten
White baking chocolate curls and lemon peel strips, optional

Directions:

Preheat oven to 325ºF.

To make crust:
In a medium bowl, mix together the flour, confectioners' sugar, and peel. Then, add melted butter and use a fork to mix until crumbly. Press mixture into a 9-inch springform pan coated with cooking spray. Bake until golden (25-30 minutes). Set aside until needed.

To make filling:
With an electric mixer or stand mixer, beat cream cheese and sugar until smooth. Mix in white chocolate, flour, lemon juice, heavy cream, lemon peel, and vanilla until smooth. Gradually add eggs until just combined.

Pour entire mixture into the prepared crust and spread evenly. Smooth with a spatula.

To bake: Set cake pan on top of aluminum foil and wrap foil around sides. Place cake pan in a large roasting pan. Add enough boiling water to the roasting pan so that the water is about halfway up the cake pan (the aluminum foil prevents water from reaching cake).

Bake in preheated oven for about 70 minutes. Cheesecake will be jiggly and will firm upon cooling, so do not over cook. Let cool for 15 minutes, then run a thin spatula around the inside rim. Chill in refrigerator for 6 hours.

Remove from springform pan and transfer to cake plate. Slice with a knife dipped in warm water for smooth cuts.

Low Sugar Cheesecake

On a diet? Or, are you looking for a delicious diabetic dessert? This low-sugar cheesecake is perfect! By skipping the crust, and adding a sugar substitute, you can satisfy your sweet tooth with out sacrificing flavor.

Total Time: 10 hours & 15 Minutes
Prep Time: 30 Minutes

Yield: 1 9-inch cheesecake
Level: Easy

Ingredients:

Pie Filling:
3 (8 ounce) packages cream cheese, at room temperature
1 cup extra-fine whole milk ricotta cheese (to refine, process in a food processor for 1 minute)
½ cup sour cream
1½ cups sugar substitute (ex: Splenda)
⅓ cup heavy cream
1 tbsp no sugar added vanilla extract
1 tbsp fresh lemon juice
2 eggs
3 egg yolks

Directions:

Preheat oven to 400°F.

In a roasting pan that can fit your 9-inch cake pan, pour 1-inch of water. Place in center of oven to preheat.

With an electric mixer or stand mixer, beat cream cheese until smooth. Mix in ricotta, sugar substitute, and ricotta until smooth.

Whisk together heavy cream, lemon juice, eggs, egg yolks, and vanilla in a separate bowl. Slowly pour this mixture into the cream cheese mixture until just combined. Do not over mix.

Pour entire mixture into a greased 9-inch springform pan. Place in heated water bath and bake for 15 minutes. Decrease over to 275°F and continue to bake for 1 hour and 30 minutes or until light golden. Turn oven off and leave cake in oven for 3 more hours. Then refrigerate for at least 5 hours.

Remove from springform pan and transfer to cake plate. Slice with a knife dipped in warm water for smooth cuts.

Chocolate Chip Cookie Dough Cheesecake

Are you looking to surprise the little ones with a treat? Try out this cheesecake with dollops of cookie dough right in the center of the filling. It is delicious… even for the parents!

Total Time: 7 hours & 25 Minutes
Prep Time: 25 Minutes

Yield: 1 9-inch cheesecake
Level: Hard

Ingredients:

Crust:
1¾ cups crushed chocolate chip cookies or chocolate wafer crumbs
¼ cup sugar
⅓ cup butter, melted

Filling:
3 (8 ounces) packages cream cheese, at room temperature
1 cup sugar
1 cup (8 ounces) sour cream
½ tsp vanilla extract
3 eggs, lightly beaten

Cookie dough:
¼ cup butter, softened
¼ cup sugar
¼ cup packed brown sugar
1 tbsp water
1 tsp vanilla extract

½ cup all-purpose flour
1½ cups mini semisweet chocolate chips, divided

Directions:

Preheat oven to 350ºF.

To make crust:
Use a fork to mix cookie crumbs and sugar in a small bowl. Mix in butter. Press mixture into a 9-inch springform pan coated with cooking spray. Place on baking sheet and set aside until needed.

To make filling:
With an electric mixer or stand mixer, beat cream cheese and sugar until smooth. Add vanilla and sour cream until well combined. Gradually add eggs until just mixed. Pour over crust and set aside.

To make cookie dough:
In a medium bowl, beat butter and sugars until very creamy. Mix in water and vanilla. Slowly beat in flour until well combined. Stir 1 cup of chocolate chips.

Use a teaspoon to drop dough over filling. Gently push dough into cheese mixture so that is it covered by the filling. Place the baking sheet in the oven and bake for 50 minutes until center is almost set. Cool for 10 minutes, then run a thin spatula around the inside rim. Chill in refrigerator for 6 hours.

Remove from springform pan and transfer to cake plate. Slice with a knife dipped in warm water for smooth cuts.

Honey Cheesecake

So simple, yet so delicious. This traditional cheesecake with a little added honey is a perfectly subtle addition to add a small twist to your basic recipe.

Total Time: 8 hours & 5 minutes
Prep Time: 20 minutes

Yield: 1 9-inch cheesecake
Level: Easy

Ingredients:

Crust:
1¾ cups graham cracker crumbs
3 tbsp light brown sugar
½ tsp ground cinnamon
½ cup melted butter

Pie Filling:
2 (8-ounce) packages of cream cheese, at room temperature
⅔ cup honey
4 eggs
1 tsp vanilla

Directions:

Preheat oven to 350°F.

To make crust:
In a medium bowl, use a fork to mix together the graham cracker crumbs, sugar, and cinnamon. Then, add the melted butter and mix well. Press mixture into a 9-inch springform pan coated with cooking spray. Set aside until needed.

To make filling:
With an electric mixer or stand mixer, beat cream cheese until smooth. Mix in honey and vanilla. Gradually add eggs until just combined.

Pour entire mixture into the prepared crust and spread evenly. Smooth with a spatula.

To bake:
Set cake pan on top of aluminum foil and wrap foil around sides. Place cake pan in a large roasting pan. Add enough boiling water to the roasting pan so that the water is about halfway up the cake pan (the aluminum foil prevents water from reaching cake).

Bake in preheated oven for 1 hour and 30 minutes. Cheesecake will be jiggly and will firm upon cooling, so do not over cook. Let cool for 15 minutes, then run a thin spatula around the inside rim. Chill in refrigerator for 6 hours.

Remove from springform pan and transfer to cake plate. Slice with a knife dipped in warm water for smooth cuts.

Pomegranate-Glazed Orange Cheesecake

It is always exciting to see at your local grocery store that pomegranates are back in season. This delicious fruit has so many possibilities. The orange cheesecake filling topped with a pomegranate-glaze make this cheesecake a perfect dessert.

Total Time: 13 hours & 30 Minutes
Prep Time: 45 Minutes

Yield: 1 9-inch cheesecake
Level: Intermediate

Ingredients

Crust:
1 cup vanilla wafer crumbs
¼ cup ground toasted almonds
2 tbsp sugar
5 tbsp butter, melted

Pie Filling:
2 (8-ounce) packages cream cheese, at room temperature
1 (8-ounce) tub mascarpone
½ cup sugar
½ cup whipping cream
4 eggs
Grated zest of 1 orange

Glaze:
2 tsp cornstarch
2 cups pomegranate juice, divided

1 tbsp sugar
2 tbsp pomegranate seeds

Directions:

Preheat oven to 350ºF.

To make crust:
In a medium bowl, use a fork to mix together the vanilla wafer crumbs, almonds, and sugar. Then, add the melted butter and mix well. Press mixture into a 9-inch springform pan coated with cooking spray. Bake until golden (about 10 minutes). Set aside until needed.

To make filling:
With an electric mixer or stand mixer, beat cream cheese until smooth. Mix in mascarpone and sugar until well combined. Gradually add eggs. Stir in zest.

Pour entire mixture into the prepared crust and spread evenly. Smooth with a spatula.

To bake: Set cake pan on top of aluminum foil and wrap foil around sides. Place cake pan in a large roasting pan. Add enough boiling water to the roasting pan so that the water is about halfway up the cake pan (the aluminum foil prevents water from reaching cake).

Bake in preheated oven for 65 minutes. Cheesecake will be jiggly and will firm upon cooling, so do not over cook. Let cool for 15 minutes, then run a thin spatula around the inside rim. Chill in refrigerator for 4 hours.

To make glaze:

In a small bowl, mix cornstarch and 2 tbsp pomegranate juice. Set aside.

In a saucepan, bring remaining pomegranate juice and sugar to a boil. Reduce heat and simmer until liquid is reduced to ¾ cup (about 20 minutes). Mix in cornstarch mixture and simmer until thickened (about 2 minutes).

Bring glaze to room temperature.

Remove cake from springform pan and transfer to cake plate. Pour over glaze over chilled cake and garnish with pomegranate seeds. Slice with a knife dipped in warm water for smooth cuts.

Bailey's™ Irish Cream Cheesecake

This cheesecake is almost too good to be true! What is even more delicious than a creamy cheesecake? One with the smooth taste of Bailey's added! An Oreo crust, coffee whipped topping, and Bailey's center create a delicious combo that you will be dying to try again.

Total Time: 8 hours & 5 minutes
Prep Time: 30 Minutes

Yield: 1 9-inch cheesecake
Level: Intermediate

Ingredients

Crust:
½ cup toasted pecans, cooled and crushed
2 cups chocolate Oreo cookie crumbs
¼ cup sugar
6 tbsp melted butter

Filling:
2¼ lbs cream cheese, at room temperature
1⅔ cups sugar
5 eggs, at room temp
1 cup Baileys Original Irish Cream
1 tbsp vanilla
1 cup semi-sweet chocolate chips

Coffee Cream Topping
1 cup chilled whipping cream
2 tbsp sugar
1 tsp instant coffee powder

Chocolate curls or Heath Bar crumbles, for decoration on top if desired

Directions:

Preheat oven to 375ºF.

To make crust:
In a medium bowl, use a fork to mix together all crust ingredients. Press mixture into a 10-inch springform pan coated with cooking spray. Bake for 7-10 minutes. Set aside to let cool.

Reduce oven to 325ºF.

To make filling:
With an electric mixer or stand mixer, beat cream cheese until smooth. Gradually add sugar and eggs until combined. Beat in Bailey's and vanilla until smooth.

Sprinkle half the chocolate chips over cooled crust.

Pour entire mixture into the prepared crust and spread evenly. Smooth with a spatula. Sprinkle remaining chocolate chips.

To bake:
Set cake pan on top of aluminum foil and wrap foil around sides. Place cake pan in a large roasting pan. Add enough boiling water to the roasting pan so that the water is about halfway up the cake pan (the aluminum foil prevents water from reaching cake).

Bake in preheated oven for 1 hour and 20 minutes. Cheesecake will be jiggly and will firm upon cooling, so do not over cook. Let cool for 15 minutes, then run a thin spatula around the inside rim. Chill in refrigerator for 6 hours.

Remove from springform pan and transfer to cake plate. Slice with a knife dipped in warm water for smooth cuts.

To make coffee cream topping:
Mix all ingredients until smooth. Spread over cooled cake. Top with chocolate curls or Heath Bar if desired.

Kahlúa™ Chocolate Cheesecake

Imagine a creamy cheesecake, complimented with a delicious coffee liqueur. Okay, stop imagining and start tasting! This Kahlúa Chocolate Cheesecake is truly delicious. Any adult will enjoy the flavor Kahlúa brings to the cream cheese center.

Total Time: 7 hours & 14 Minutes
Prep Time: 24 minutes

Yield: 1 9-inch cheesecake
Level: Intermediate

Ingredients

Crust:
1⅓ cups chocolate wafer crumbs
¼ cup softened butter
1 tbsp sugar

Filling:
2 (8 ounce) packages cream cheese, at room temperature
1½ cups semi-sweet chocolate chips
1/4 cup Kahlua or 1/4 cup coffee-flavored liqueur
2 tbsp butter
2 eggs, beaten
⅓ cup sugar
¼ tsp salt
1 cup sour cream

Directions:

Preheat oven to 350°F.

To make crust:
In a medium bowl, use a fork to mix together all crust ingredients. Press mixture into a 9-inch springform pan coated with cooking spray. Set aside until needed.

To make filling:
Using a small saucepan, melt chocolate and butter. Add Kahula. Stir until smooth and set aside.

With an electric mixer or stand mixer, beat cream cheese until smooth. Add sugar, salt and sour cream until combined. Gradually add eggs.

Slowly mix in chocolate mixture until smooth.

Pour entire mixture into the prepared crust and spread evenly. Smooth with a spatula.

To bake: Set cake pan on top of aluminum foil and wrap foil around sides. Place cake pan in a large roasting pan. Add enough boiling water to the roasting pan so that the water is about halfway up the cake pan (the aluminum foil prevents water from reaching cake).

Bake in preheated oven for 40 minutes. Cheesecake will be jiggly and will firm upon cooling, so do not over cook. Let cool for 15 minutes, then run a thin spatula around the inside rim. Chill in refrigerator for 6 hours.

Remove from springform pan and transfer to cake plate. Garnish with whipped cream and chocolate shavings if desired. Slice with a knife dipped in warm water for smooth cuts.

So, how did it go?

Did you try a recipe? Did you try all 37 recipes? Either way - did you love it?

Hopefully, you made a delicious cheesecake and ate your heart out. After "wowing" your guests, be sure to try more! Plus, don't forget to get your free gift for even more exciting recipes.

By now, you have realized just how easy (and delicious) making cheesecakes can be. If you are feeling generous, maybe you shared a recipe or two with your mother... you know, so she can try to make cheesecake as savory as yours!

I would love to hear how your cheesecake adventure went. Email me your successes, your struggles, your questions, and your ideas!

Thank you again for being awesome and buying this book!

Here's to you and your cooking adventures,

Jennifer Connor

Printed in Great Britain
by Amazon